COLORING BOOK TO

- - - - - - - - - - - -

- - - - - - - - - - - -

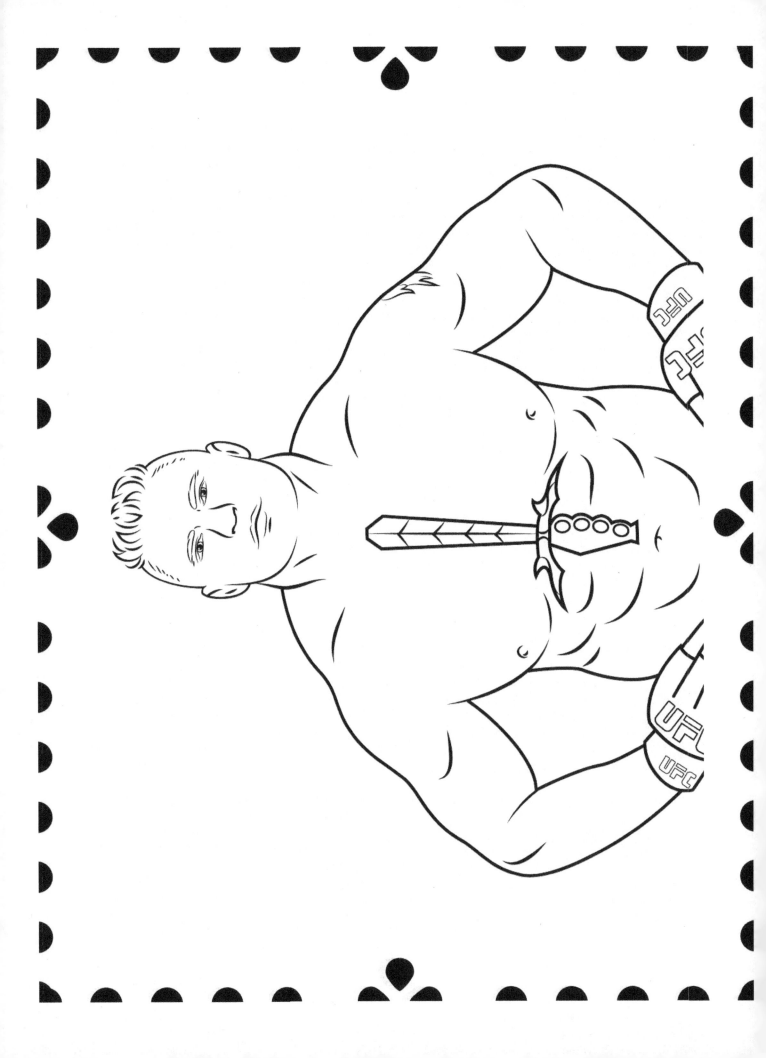

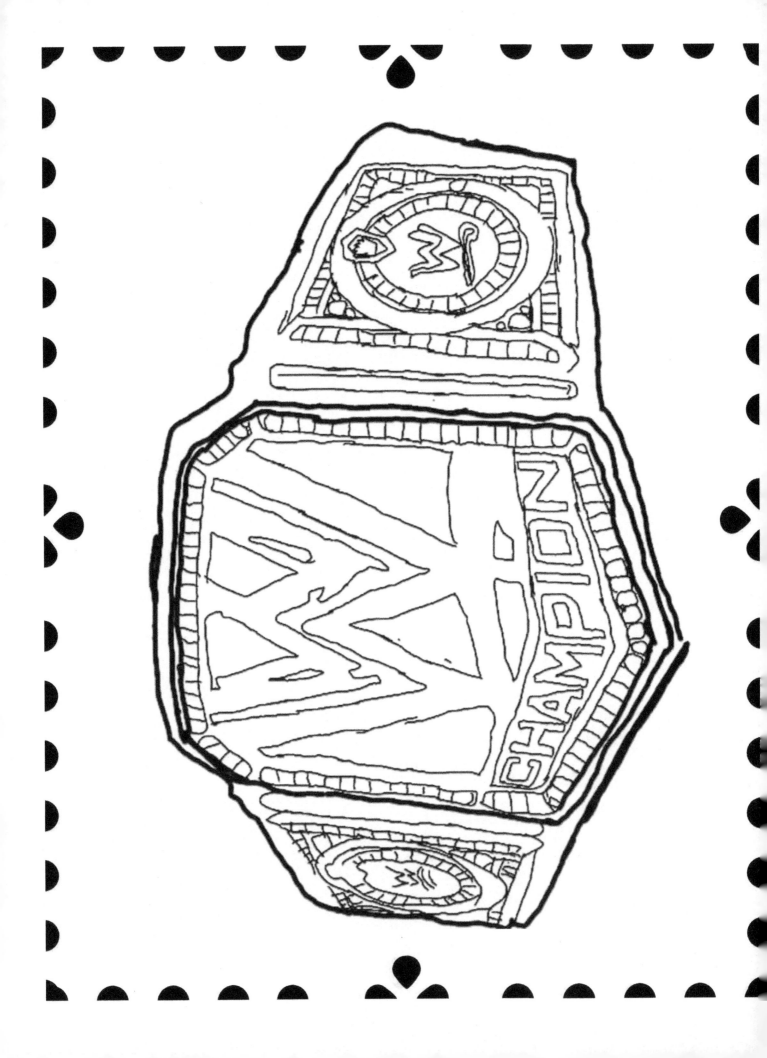

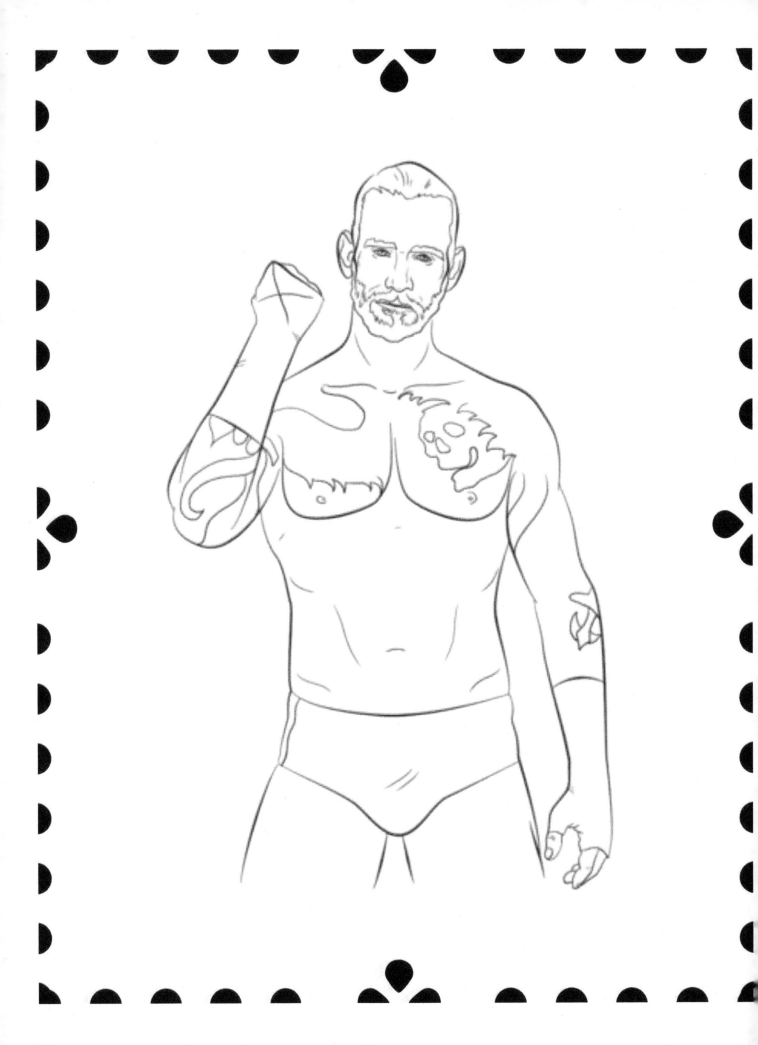

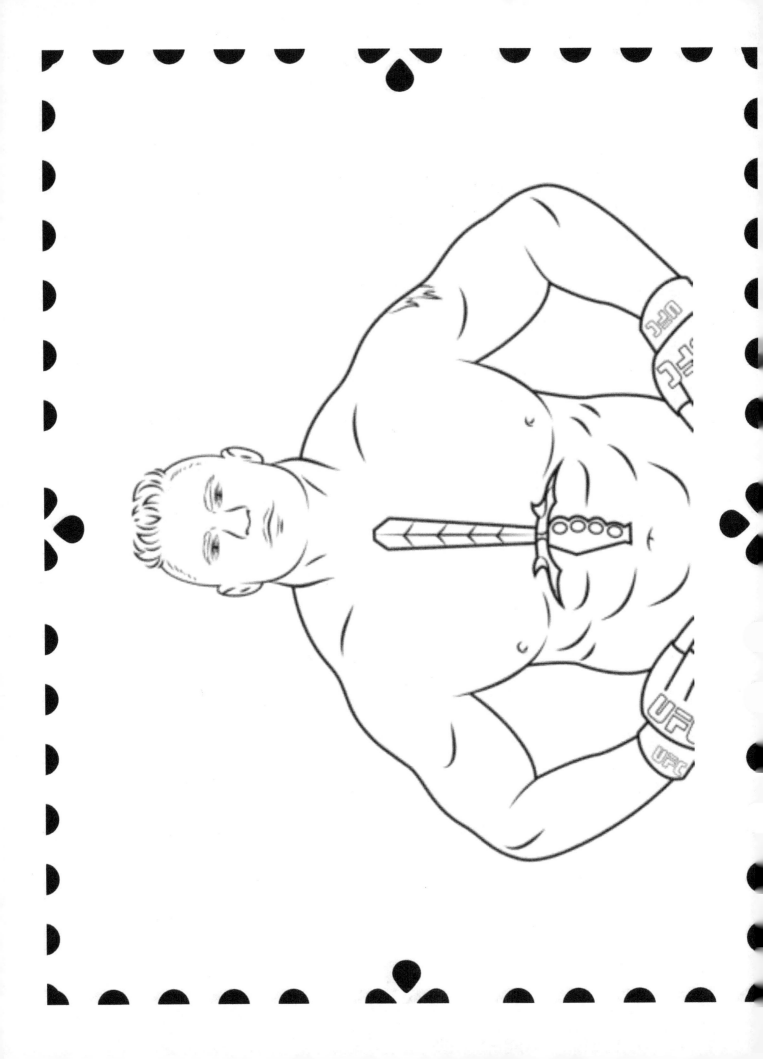

DRAW HERE WHAT YOU LEARNED

DRAW HERE WHAT YOU LEARNED

DRAW HERE WHAT YOU LEARNED

DRAW HERE WHAT YOU LEARNED

DRAW HERE WHAT YOU LEARNED

DRAW HERE WHAT YOU LEARNED

DRAW HERE WHAT YOU LEARNED

DRAW HERE WHAT YOU LEARNED

DRAW HERE WHAT YOU LEARNED

DRAW HERE WHAT YOU LEARNED

DRAW HERE WHAT YOU LEARNED

DRAW HERE WHAT YOU LEARNED

DRAW HERE WHAT YOU LEARNED

DRAW HERE WHAT YOU LEARNED

DRAW HERE WHAT YOU LEARNED

Made in the USA
Middletown, DE
10 December 2024

66590794R00057